Life's Lessons
for Children

(and for teachers
and parents, too!)

❧

Janice Loschiavo, M.A., R.N.
Illustrations by Richard William Loschiavo

FCP

Full Court Press
Englewood Cliffs, New Jersey

First Edition

Copyright © 2016 by Janice Loschiavo

Published in the United States of America
by Full Court Press, 601 Palisade Avenue,
Englewood Cliffs, NJ 07632
fullcourtpressnj.com

ISBN 978-1-938812-82-8
Library of Congress Catalog No. 2016959332

Editing and Book Design by Barry Sheinkopf for Bookshapers (bookshapers.com)

Colophon by Liz Sedlack

THIS BOOK IS DEDICATED

To all school nurses—past, present and future.
May we always remember:
Children do not interrupt our work.
They are our work.
Janice Loschiavo

And to my mom, dad,
and awesome brother, Luke.
Richard William Loschiavo

ACKNOWLEDGMENTS

Janice Loschiavo

I wish to thank Barry Sheinkopf for his patience in guiding me through the publishing process, and for his many helpful suggestions in formatting this book. He graciously shared his extensive knowledge, and I appreciate his efforts on my behalf.

I thank the ladies in my writing group—Paula Mate, Jane Paterson and Tina Segali—for their input as each story was written and expanded upon. They offered priceless wisdom and insight into this project.

I thank my terrific grandson Richard for capturing, in ink, the essence of each story so beautifully.

Richard William Loschiavo

I want to acknowledge all my wonderful teachers at Oradell Public School and thank them for helping me draw and learn.

Introduction

IF YOU'VE PICKED UP THIS BOOK, you care about children and recognize the difficulties they face in coping with their problems.

The stories in *Life Lessons for Children* were written to help parents and teachers guide youngsters in their lives to become more resilient as they cope with real-life issues at home and in school. In *Life Lessons* you will encounter children as they come face to face with issues in their elementary and high school years.

The book grew out of the more than thirty years I proudly spent as a school nurse and teacher of health education. I had the privilege to witness first hand how often students must struggle with difficult situations, how hard parents work to do a better job than their parents did and how most teachers continuously strive to guide students and parents to make appropriate decisions. As a university instructor for the last fifteen years, I also help prepare school nurses for their work in the communities they serve.

In this book, each life lesson unfolds as a story designed to provoke a stimulating, heartfelt discussion about the complex challenges growing children face. The goal of the book is to help them not only survive, but thrive in our ever more complex world.

Life Lessons is useful for character education in the home or classroom. The parent will find the scenarios helpful in opening a comfortable dialog. The teacher will see that each story helps the student develop health literacy and provokes meaningful discussions relevant to the National Health Education Standards. Critical issues such as bullying, sexual abuse and gender identity are approached in an age-appropriate manner.

Through guided discussions, students are offered the opportunity to brainstorm resolutions so when placed in a similar situation, they are empowered and capable of making a better decision. In building resilience, the child of today will better deal with the world as it is, not as it should be.

Each lesson clearly identifies:

Title
Family Member
Summary
Themes
Health Education Standard
Objectives
Pivotal Questions
Evaluation Means
Teaching Strategies
Suggested follow-up readings

Why This Book Now?

I am honored that I have had the opportunity to learn from the best; our children of today. They have inspired and enlightened me. I now have come to recognize some important facts:

- The typical American family has evolved to include many variations—all healthy, all good. Families can be blended, same sex, extended, interracial, or possess totally different belief systems.
- Educating children today is more complex than ever. The individual needs of children are recognized and addressed in a mainstreamed school setting.
- The school experience has dramatically changed over the past decade. Children can spend up to twelve

hours a day in a school environment. Very few children begin school in Kindergarten. Many are placed in day care as infants.

- Students come to school with "baggage." Their day is greatly influenced by the home environment. Some children are products of loving families but many others have never known a happy, peaceful home atmosphere. These children must find a reliable support system. Sometimes this is outside of the home. School and the people in it may represent the only constant, secure place they know and can come to for guidance. Siblings may be relied upon to help younger family members and thus lose much of their own opportunity for childhood.

THE FOLLOWING PAGES WILL present real-life scenarios typical of situations faced by children in the current, real world. The family described is not perfect and their stories do not always end happily. They mirror real life and reflect suffering as well as joy experienced by us all.

At home and at school, dedicated adults want to ensure that the children in our care get what they need. As a mother and grandmother with three adult children and six, happy, healthy grandchildren, I have seen issues unfold from both sides of the desk.

My hope is that this book will help those who follow in my footsteps: teachers, parents, nurses, grandparents. May you all recognize your own needs and be available to meet the many, unique needs of today's school-aged child.

Now it is time to meet the Moore family and hear their stories. Join Jake, Katie, Michael, and Samantha, as they navigate through some of life's difficult challenges. As you watch them struggle, learn and grow, perhaps you will find even greater understanding and empathy for the child of today.

By implementing these lessons, I am certain that, at the very least, these efforts will bring comfort to educators in knowing that they have extended a warm, understanding hand to the child and guided them along the sometimes treacherous path to adulthood.

The Moore Family

The Moore family situation may seem uncommon, but it's rather representative of what's happening in America these days.

Fred Moore divorced his first wife and started another family. He's seldom seen by the children of his first wife. Jake, Katie, Michael, or Samantha have learned not to expect him to be part of their lives.

Audrey Moore is employed full time with minimum pay. She gets little financial or emotional support from her ex-husband. She met a man a year after her divorce from Fred became final, remarried, got divorced again, and has been overwhelmed ever since by her responsibilities.

Jake

Jake is a scared, confused six-year-old with Attetion Deficit Disorder.

Jake's Stories:
The Pumpkin Cried
May I Play?
A Special Day

Katie

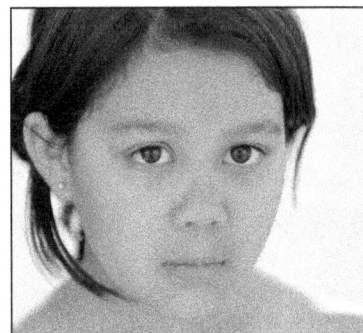

Ten-year-old Katie is a mature, caring, but sad girl.

Katie's Stories:
*They Had Nothing to Say to
Each Other*
I No Longer Find It Funny
I Could Have Told the Truth

Michael

Michael is a loner with possible gender-identity issues. He is angry and resents his father.

Michael's Stories:
The Right Thing
A Smile Crossed His Face
The Turning Point

Samantha

Sixteen-year-old Samantha is bright, beautiful, and has the responsibility of running the household.

Samantha's Stories:
Hey, Baby
*How Could You Do Such a
Foolish Thing?*
*I Never Told Anyone This
Before*

And Here Are Their Stories

YOU'LL BE READING three stories about how each of the Moore kids comes to grips with some of the really difficult challenges all children face as they grow up.

Read these stories, and become enlightened. As you read, think about the situations children face. Do they resonate with you? Have you, or your brother, sister, child, grandchild, faced a similar situation? As caring adults, it is essential that we do all we can to help the child of today.

I hope you enjoy reading and sharing these stories with children. I trust you will find them helpful in meeting the educational challenges we all face today.

Jake

The Pumpkin Cried

"No one wants me, and I know why!" Peter cried. Peter the Pumpkin was alone on the shelf at the farm stand. All the other pumpkins set down near him earlier that morning had already been bought. The farmer had moved him right up front where people could not miss him, but still no one took him home.

Earlier that day, a nice lady had picked him up to look a little closer but quickly put him back on the shelf.

The other pumpkins are a bright orange and perfectly shaped. I am neither, Peter thought, and he started to cry. It was true. He had a small top and round bottom and was more of a mustard yellow than orange color. But inside he was perfect, just like all the other pumpkins.

Halloween was the next day and just about all the other pumpkins were gone. It started to get dark and cold, and still no one had bought him to take home. Once Halloween passed, all hope would be gone. I will be thrown in the garbage can and never know what it's like to be carved out, painted, and enjoyed, thought Peter sadly.

The farmer was starting to put things away and close his stand for the night when one more car arrived. Mrs. Moore pulled it into the parking lot at the farm stand. She sat behind the wheel while Samantha and Jake got out to find a pumpkin. Jake was very excited and started running around, looking and touching all the pumpkins.

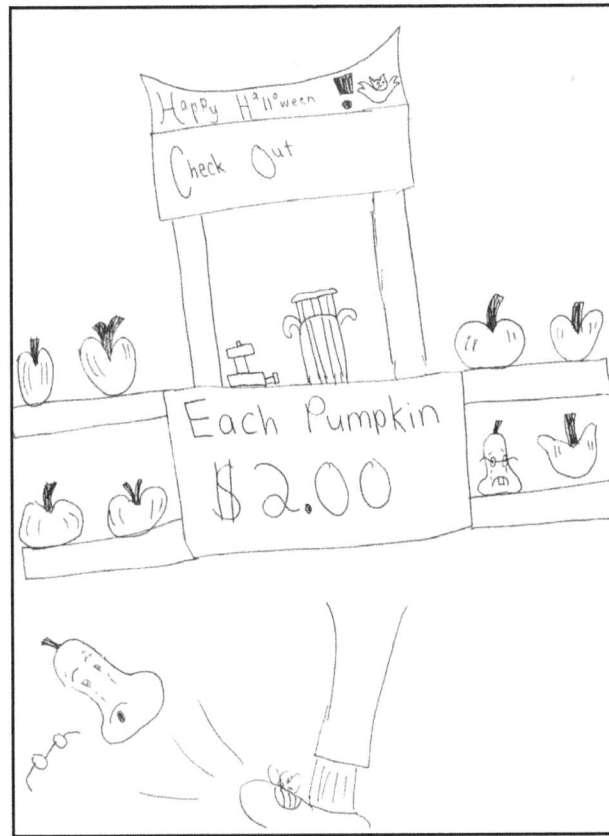

When Jake saw Peter he picked him up, stared a few seconds, and shouted, "Ugh! This pumpkin is ugly! It looks more like a pear than a pumpkin. I hate pears." He threw Peter down on the ground and kicked him.

Peter the Pumpkin rolled around on the hard ground. He was stunned and shaken. How could someone be so mean for no good reason? He couldn't help his shape and color. Inside he was the same as every other pumpkin. But as sad as Peter felt, he felt a little better that at least someone had noticed him. Even bad attention was better than no attention at all.

Jake's sister, Samantha, came running over. "What is wrong with you, Jake?" she scolded him. "If you act this way I will not get you any pumpkin for tomorrow. Now, pick up that pumpkin and see if you broke it."

Sad and embarrassed, Jake lifted Peter and brushed off the dirt. Peter was not cracked. He looked the same, but he did hurt inside.

Samantha looked closely at Peter. She said, "You know, Jake, this is really a nice pumpkin, and his yellow color will match the corn stalks outside our home. Nobody will have a pumpkin like yours."

Jake held Peter for a few moments and again looked closely at him. "You know, Samantha, I'm getting used to this pumpkin's different color. I think I like it. Can I paint eyes and a smiley face on him?"

"Of course you can," Samantha said. "I'll help you when we get home."

"I want to bring him inside at night, so he doesn't get cold. Besides, someone might steal my special pumpkin."

Samantha paid the farmer, and Jake, Samantha, and Peter the Pumpkin all got in the car to go home in time for Halloween.

Peter the Pumpkin smiled to himself. Then he started to cry again, but this time he cried happy tears.

Discussion Guide

Title: **The Pumpkin Cried**

Family Member: Jake

Themes: Respect, Prejudice

Summary: Jake wanted to buy the perfect-looking pumpkin.
He soon realized that, despite outward appearances,
all pumpkins, like people, were the same inside.

Standard: National Health Education Standards 4 and 5
*Students will demonstrate the ability to use interpersonal
communication skills to enhance health, and avoid or
reduce health risks.*
*Students will demonstrate the ability to use decision-
making skills to enhance health.*

Objectives: At the completion of the lesson, the student shall:
- Identify what it feels like to be rejected
- Describe how one feels when they are excluded/included
- Discuss the uniqueness of each person
- Recognize that each person (pumpkin) is the same inside
- List three ways people are alike and different

Pivotal Questions: Why was Peter the Pumpkin sad?
Why did no one buy Peter the Pumpkin?
How did this make Peter feel?
How was Peter the same as/different from the other Pumpkins?
Did any of you ever feel that you were not wanted?
Have you ever seen someone hurt a person as Jake did to Peter?
Why was Peter a little happy even after he was kicked?
Why did Peter's sister get angry with Jake?

Did Jake know that Peter was hurt inside?
How can you tell if you hurt someone's feelings?
Why was Peter crying at the beginning/end of the story?

Evaluation: Evaluation shall be in terms of the student's ability to participate in a meaningful discussion, relate the story to their own experiences and complete the hands-on activity to the best of their ability.

Strategies: Read the story to the class.
Reread the story again and pause to ask the pivotal questions at appropriate times.
Have students return to their desks and, depending on artistic and writing ability, allow students to:

- Draw a picture of a sad and happy pumpkin.
- Create their own picture book with words describing the action.
- Write and illustrate the story from the store owner or child buying the pumpkin's perspective.
- Write and illustrate a story of an incident of prejudice they witnessed.
- Ask students to share their pictures/stories with the rest of the class.
- Close and summarize the lesson by reading one of the recommended story books.

Follow-up Readings:

Andreae, Giles. (2001). *Giraffes can't dance*. Guy Parker-Rees Orchard Books.

Snorynory. (2009). *The lioness and snail*. Free audio and downloadable stories.

Kates, Bobbi. (2015) *We're different, we're the same*. Sesame Street Picture Books.

May I Play?

PULLING THE *STAR WARS* COM-FORTER over his head, Jake closed his eyes and pretended he was sleeping. He could hear low voices coming from the kitchen and smell the morning coffee and burnt toast. Secure in his little world, he rolled over and tried to grab a few more minutes of sleep.

But Jake could not go back to sleep. At first he could not remember what it was, but he knew today was special. With sleepy eyes, he looked around the room. There at the foot of his bed were his clothes. *Oh, no*, the summer vacation was over and today he had to go to school! They had just moved, and he had to start in a new class and a new school. He wouldn't know anyone in his class, or the whole school for that matter. Jake knew he didn't understand numbers or how to read at all. The work had been hard for him in Kindergarten last year, but at least it was only for a half day and he had friends. Now he had to go to first grade, and he was alone. This was not a good thing to think about.

"Let's *go*, Jake," his mother yelled. "Time to get up."

Jake moaned, "I can't. I'm sick. I just threw up. Smell my breath. I am sick, *very* sick."

"Don't make me late for work. Your brother is already dressed, and he's going to walk you to school." She yanked off his comforter. "Get moving, *now!*"

Still, Jake did not move. He pulled up the cover again and snuggled under his comforter.

After a few minutes, Michael came running into the room. "Come on, Jake. You're making me late too, and I'll get into trouble. Mom is gone, and I just do not have time to *fight* with you."

Michael was really annoyed that he had to take his brother to school and was already late for his first day. As a high school student, Michael would get in trouble, but Jake would not. It was just not fair.

Michael gave Jake one last reminder, and finally threatened to leave without him, before Jake got up and dressed.

Michael walked Jake into the building and together they found the main office. Children were already seated in their rooms, and the first day of school was well under way. A friendly lady asked Jake who his teacher was. Jake remembered it was Mrs. Ramos, and the nice lady showed him where the room was.

Terrified, Jake stared up at Michael. Michael squeezed his little brother's hand, bent down, and whispered, "I'm scared too. You'll be fine. I'll be back to get you after school."

Jake opened the classroom door and stood there for a second while the teacher finished speaking to the circle of children seated on the carpet. Mrs. Ramos looked over at Jake and immediately came toward him. Smiling, she said, "You must be Jake. I was waiting for you. All the other children are here, and I was hoping you weren't sick and had to miss your first day of school."

Mrs. Ramos explained, "I was just telling the class about how hard it is to leave the family we love and come to school. I told the others that we all have *another* family now, a *school* family. Please come in and meet everyone." She explained to the other children that Jake was new in the school, and she hoped they would all try to help make him feel comfortable. The children nodded, and several boys made room for Jake to sit near them on the carpet.

Jake felt much better. He really liked Mrs. Ramos, and, throughout the morning, children showed him where the boys' bathroom, water fountain, and gym were located. When lunchtime came, Mrs. Ramos walked the class to the cafeteria, said she would see them in a little while, and that they should enjoy lunch and recess.

Jake sat down at one of the tables where the other boys in his class were. Immediately, someone asked him to move so he could sit next to his friend. Jake moved several times to make room for other children and finally wound up at the end of the table, with the girls in the class separating him from the rest of the boys.

After lunch, the children were allowed to play outside. Jake sat on a bench and waited to be asked to play. When no one invited him, he tried to join some boys playing soccer. "May I play?" he asked. They told him there were too many, so he couldn't play with them. The boy who had let him sit near him in class told him that, since he was new, he really didn't know the rules anyway. Jake almost started to cry and walked over to sit on the bench again, alone.

Jake soon got tired of watching the others and decided he would play on the monkey bars with some other boys from his class. As he approached them he heard them say, "Let's run away from Jake." Confused, Jake returned to the bench and sat down to wait for the teacher.

When the bell finally rang for them to go back inside, Jake was relieved. Inside the classroom, the children were once again nice to him.

The next day, Jake didn't want to go to school. He cried and said he was sick. After his mom left for work, he told his brother what had happened at recess. Michael felt terrible for him. Michael understood that the children were just being nice because the teacher was in the room. Outside, they didn't care and just wanted to play with their friends. Michael explained to Jake that it would take time, but that he would have friends, too. Michael told Jake to get dressed quickly. He had a plan and promised Jake that today would be better.

Michael and Jake arrived early, well before the children had to line up to enter the building. Michael brought a soccer ball with him, and he and Jake started playing the way they always did. Jake was really good at soccer, and the other kids soon noticed. A few of Jake's classmates started watching them and soon asked Michael if they could play, too. Michael told them to ask Jake, since it was his ball. "May I play?" they each asked Jake, just as the bell rang and they had to line up to go into school.

"Sure, we can play during lunchtime recess," Jake told them.

When lunchtime came, the other boys were eager to sit near Jake. Jake made sure that all the boys were sitting together, and that he wasn't leaving anyone out. They had a lot of fun playing soccer during recess. Jake let everyone play.

The next morning, Jake was up, dressed, and ready for school. He knew he would still have to work hard at his numbers and reading, but he really looked forward to going to school, letting Mrs. Ramos teach him, and playing with his new friends.

Discussion Guide

Title:	**May I Play?**
Family Member:	Jake
Themes:	Kindness, Compassion, Fairness
Summary:	Children must have people they can rely on. When parents are unavailable, they look to others to support their needs. When Jake has a difficult time the first day of school, his big brother Michael comes to his rescue.
Standard:	National Health Education Standard 7 *All students will demonstrate the ability to practice health-enhancing behaviors, and avoid or reduce risks.*
Objectives:	At the completion of the lesson, the learner shall:

- Describe how it feels to be in a new situation.
- Recognize the feeling associated with being excluded
- Identify three ways to make someone feel part of a group
- Differentiate between sincere and insincere behaviors.
- Prepare how to handle difficult situations.

Pivotal Questions: How did Jake feel on his first day at school?

Why was Jake scared?

What did Jake's teacher, Mrs. Ramos, say to him when he got to the classroom?

How did the other children treat Jake in the lunchroom?

Why do you think they were nice in the classroom and not so nice in the lunchroom?

Why did the children refuse to let Jake play?

What could the children have done to make Jake feel better?
How did Jake's big brother fix the problem?
Who else could have helped Jake?

Evaluation: Evaluation shall be in terms of provoking a meaningful
discussion and the students' ability to relate the story
to their own experiences.

Activities: Read the story to the class.
Reread the story again and pause to
    ask the pivotal questions at appropriate times.
Have the students return to their desks and, depending on their
    ability and choice, have them write a story about a time they
    felt excluded and how the situation was handled.
Draw a picture of Jake in the classroom and then on the
    playground the first day and second day.
Allow the students to share their pictures or stories with the class.

Follow-up Readings:

Long, Ethan. (2013). *Chamelia and the new kid in class.* Hachette
    Book Group.
Thaler, Mike. (2014). *The Teacher from the Black Lagoon,*
    illustrated by Jareen Lee. Scholastic Books.

A Special Day

JAKE WAS PLAYING with his pencil. Actually, he wasn't really playing. With deadly force, he was taking his newly sharpened pencil and slamming it hard into the little package of tissues he had in his desk. Jake was *angry*. He'd forgotten to bring his new colored-pencil box to school with him that morning. It was his prize for being good all last week, and he wanted to show his friend, David.

Jake looked up to see his teacher, Mrs. Ramos, staring at him. "Put it away and pay attention," she said calmly.

Jake did as he was told, pausing only an instant to clench his fist and punch the side of his desk. The first-grader turned his head so he could see his friend David and his classmates. The others were all listening with polite attention to Mrs. Ramos. Jake didn't care about anything she was saying, but he *wanted* to care. It seemed that, no matter how hard he tried, after just a few minutes of doing or listening, he got angry and wanted to do something else. Usually by the time he thought about what he wanted to do, he had already done it.

The cheerful classroom faced east, bathing the room in morning sunlight. Bulletin boards surrounded the eighteen children, boasting beautiful, original work of each student, laminated and carefully hung. Desks were neatly arranged in groups of four.

Jake's desk faced the teacher's corner

desk—all day. He had to wiggle and turn to see his friends. Whenever he did, Mrs. Ramos told him to turn around and pay attention.

Early in the school year it was decided that the other children were a distraction, and Jake needed help concentrating and controlling his anger. So he was being separated from the other students.

Today was a special day. They were getting ready for parents to visit in the classroom, and Jake's mom was coming. She said she would take her lunch hour a little early, so she could be there by eleven to watch with the other parents. Today, he needed to be good.

"Make Mom proud," his sister had begged him that morning before leaving for school.

Jake put the pencil and tissue pack down. He was not off to a good start.

A few minutes before eleven, the parents started arriving. Jake's mom was there, too.

They took seats in the back of the room, smiled, and listened quietly as Mrs. Ramos gave a reading lesson. After a few minutes, the class was told to move to the carpet. They all had assigned areas where to sit. Jake gladly joined the others in the reading circle. Here he was not separated. Here he could see the other children.

More parents came, and the room started getting crowded. A mom walked in with a little boy about two years old. By now all the seats in the back were taken. This new mom had no place to go, so she quietly sat at Jake's desk, putting her little boy on her lap.

Jake did not mind. He just wished he could get up and give the boy a toy to play with. He knew what it was like to have to try and sit when you just couldn't.

After just a few minutes, circle time was over, and the children had to return to their desks. Mrs. Ramos told Jake to sit at the desk of an absent child. Relieved to be with the other children, Jake gladly sat where he was told.

Jake's mom smiled at him, and he smiled back.

Mrs. Ramos started passing out a work sheet and telling the children to match up the words with the pictures. Jake did his work quietly and was one of the first finished. He folded his hands to keep them from moving and looked up at Mrs. Ramos. Both of them were surprised.

When it was almost lunchtime, the parents started to leave. From his new seat, Jake smiled again at his mom and waved. He knew he had made her proud. He sat quietly, hoping Mrs. Ramos would not notice and make him move back to his lonely seat. She didn't, and the class started to get ready for lunch.

Lunch was great. The day was sunny and warm, so recess was outdoors. It was Jake's favorite time of day.

Jake had decided that, when he went back to class, he would just sit down at the other desk and hope Mrs. Ramos wouldn't make him move back to his seat by her desk.

He was hanging his coat up in the hall locker when Mrs. Ramos came over to him. "Jake," she said, "I hope you don't mind, but I moved your desk next to David's. I think you'll be happier there. I'm keeping an extra place next to me, just in case there are times you can't pay attention and need a quieter spot. When you think you're ready, you can move back next to David. Is that OK with you?"

"Yes!" was all he could say.

Jake joyfully went into the class and found his new place. He put his hand into his desk, searching for his tissues, and felt something hard. Pulling it out, he saw his new colored pencil box. Mom must have noticed that he'd forgotten it and brought it in for him while they were at recess.

Yes, today was a special day, and one Jake would never forget.

Discussion Guide

Title:	**A Special Day**
Family Member:	Jake
Themes:	Acceptance, Self-Esteem, Fairness
Summary:	Jake has Attention Deficit Disorder with Hyperactivity. His actions cause such disruption in the class that the teacher has placed him at a desk in front of her so she can continuously monitor his behavior. Jake is unhappy and resents this placement until one day when he proves he is capable of better classroom behavior.
Standard:	National Health Education Standard 5 *Students will demonstrate the ability to use decision-making skills to enhance health.*
Objectives:	At the completion of the lesson, the student shall:

- Recognize how actions produce consequences
- Appreciate that good behavior will be rewarded
- Identify behaviors that will be acceptable in a classroom
- Demonstrate understanding of individual differences

Pivotal Questions: How do you think Jake felt sitting away from the other children?

Why was Jake angry?

What was special about the colored-pencil box?

What do you think Jake did that made his teacher put his desk right in front of her facing away from his friends?

Do you think Jake was bad?

Why did Jake have to move to another desk?
What made the teacher allow him to stay in the new seat?
Do you think Jake will be able to stay sitting next to David?
How did Mrs. Ramos show that she understood Jake?

Evaluation: Evaluation shall be in terms of the student's ability to have
a meaningful discussion and demonstrate understanding of
differences of all.

Strategies: Divide the class into groups of three or four.
Give each group time to discuss and role play the story.
Have the students draw a picture of Jake coloring with his
new pencil box.
Have the students draw a picture of the things that are
special to them.

Follow-up Readings:

You Tube Video, We Do Listen Foundation. *Howard B. Wiggle
bottom Learns to Listen: books, songs, lessons.*
Griffith, Holly. (2014). *Back to School with Howard B. Wigglebot
tom.* We Do Listen Foundation.

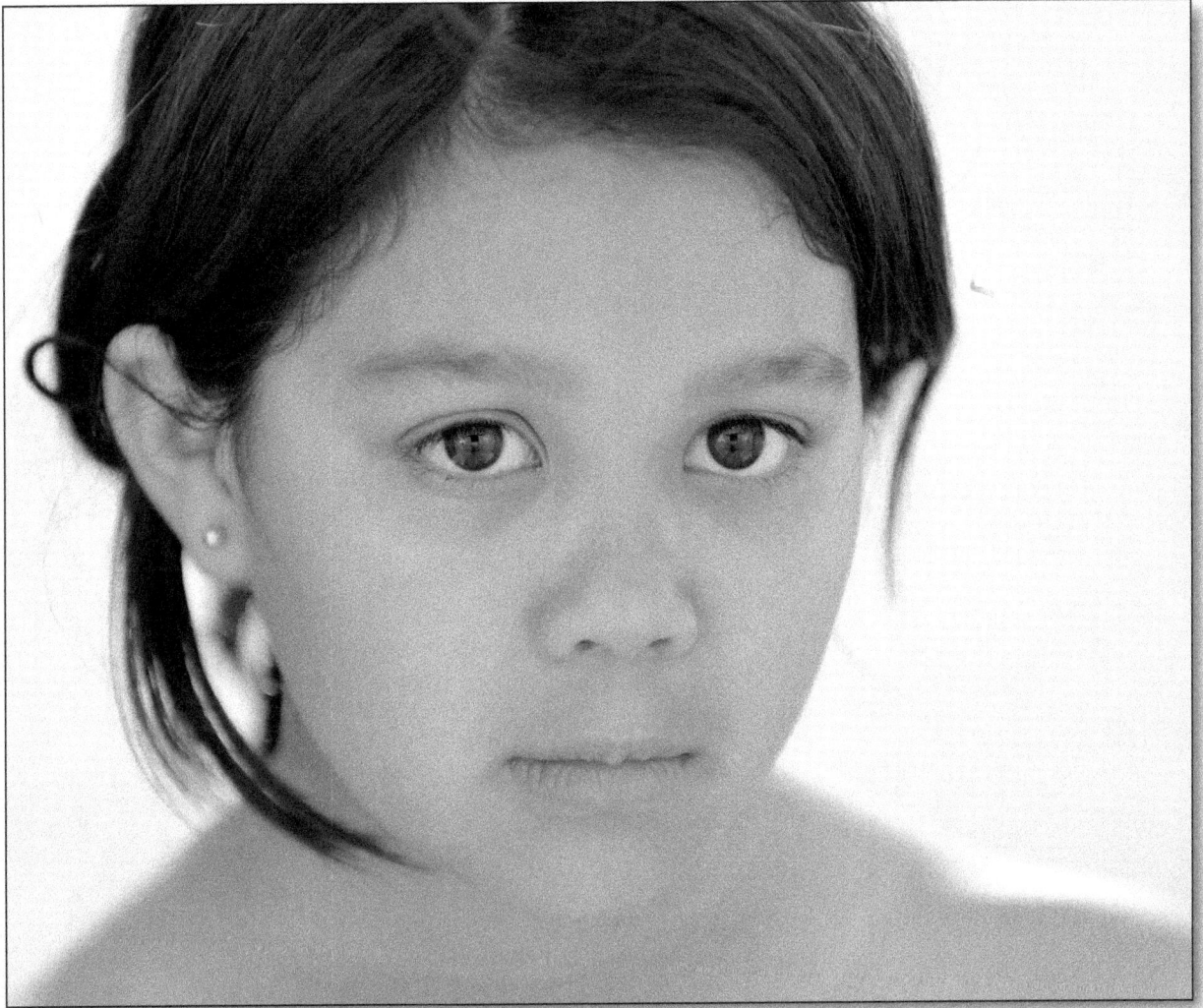

Katie

They Had Nothing to Say to Each Other. . .

KATIE GLANCED AROUND the schoolyard as the other children began to arrive. The younger ones were holding their parents' hands tightly, and groups of joyful kids were spilling out of cars. Some posed for pictures with new teachers and showed off their just-bought outfits for the first day of school. Happy reunions with teachers, parents, and children surrounded Katie. The too-short summer had ended abruptly.

Katie smiled, too. She was glad to be back and excited about fourth grade. She had heard nice things about her new teacher and never had problems with schoolwork. It was going to be a good year.

Looking around the school yard, Katie patiently waited for the one person she had desperately missed all summer. Her best friend, Emma, had been away almost the entire time, and the few opportunities they'd had for a play date had just not worked out.

Out of the corner of her eye, Katie noticed Staci and quickly pretended to be looking in her binder. Staci always wanted to be with her and Emma. Staci was OK, but Emma and Katie preferred to be alone.

Katie was clutching a note she had written to Emma. For the past two years, actually since they had learned to write in first grade, the girls had been sending notes to each other. The little letters shared special secrets and plans they had together. They would leave them in each other's pockets or slip them in their desks. It was their own way of communicating and assuring each other that they were best friends.

At last, Katie saw her. Emma had actually been standing only a few feet away from her, but Katie did not recognize her. Emma had gotten so tall, and so very pretty. Her hair was no longer in pig tails but layered pixie-like around her face. She had on a cute cut-off top and sparkle sneakers. Katie looked at her own clothes and felt she looked like a baby.

Emma was talking to a sixth-grade boy they knew. Both were laughing about something. Katie waited until the boy walked off and ran up to Emma.

Emma gave Katie a warm smile and asked if she'd had a good summer. Katie nodded and said she had missed her, and handed her the note. Emma thanked her and started talking to some other girls.

When the bell rang, the students lined up and went into the school. Emma was not in Katie's class that year, but Katie knew they would see each other at lunch. She waited anxiously, certain that Emma would have written back a note to her.

When she finally did see Emma, there was no note. There was hardly even a hello. Emma was nice enough to her but seemed much more interested in her new classmates, the girls and boys. Katie was heartbroken.

In the days ahead, Katie asked many times whether they could play after school together, but Emma always had something to do—cheerleading practice, football game she had to see, homework with her classmates.

Finally, one day, Emma agreed to play with her, and Katie was thrilled.

Emma came to Katie's house, but things were different. Emma was no longer interested in stuffed animals, Barbie dolls, or even board games. The afternoon dragged on.

Katie began to see that things had changed. They still liked each other and were friends, but it wasn't the same. They no longer exchanged notes, for one. There was no need to, since they had nothing to say to each other.

Katie was sad for a long time. She would sit quietly in her room at night and think about how much she missed Emma. Katie understood that Emma had changed and grown up faster than she had. She did not miss the Emma of today but the friendship she had had with the Emma of the past. Katie realized now that the past was gone and would never come back.

That night, Katie took out her favorite pen and pad and wrote a little note to Staci. She could leave it in her locker first thing in the morning. Katie smiled, knowing Staci would be thrilled and would quickly write her back.

Things were not the same with Emma but she had such nice memories of good times together. Maybe there would be good times with Staci ahead. Maybe even with some of the boys.

Discussion Guide

Title: ***They Had Nothing to Say to Each Other***

Family Member: Katie

Themes: Growing up, Loneliness

Summary: Katie and Emma have been best friends since Kindergarten but now have little in common. Katie longs for the relationship that once was but must learn to move on.

Standard: National Health Education Standard 4
Students will demonstrate the ability to use interpersonal communication skills to enhance health, and avoid or reduce health risks.

Objectives: At the completion of the lesson, the student will:
- Describe three physical and emotional changes associated with adolescence
- Recognize that it is normal to mature at different rates
- Develop strategies to deal with disappointment

Pivotal Questions: What was special about Katie and Emma's friendship?
Why did Emma not want to play with Katie?
Do you think that Emma hates Katie?
How does Katie handle Emma not wanting to be with her?
What does Katie decide to do?
Do you still have the same friends you had when you were younger?

Evaluation: Evaluation shall be in terms of the student recognizing and finding comfort in knowing that as they mature, meet, and learn from others, they will find more friends that they have much in common with.

Strategies: Read the story of Katie and Emma.
Re-read the story, and ask the pivotal questions.
Have the students write this story from Emma's point of view.
Break the students into groups and give each group a scenario to discuss:

Your best friend, Tom, hasn't included you in a soccer game after school. You are disappointed and don't understand why you were excluded from a game you always play together. What should you do?

You don't want to go to the library after school with your friend. You promised, but now some others invited you to go shopping. What should you do?

A bunch of kids are all planning to go to a movie together. You want to go, but your best friend does not. What should you do?

Follow-up Readings:

Jamieson, Victoria. (2015). *Roller girl.* Penguin Young Readers.
Pyros, Andrea. (2014). *My year of epic rock.* Sourcebooks Jabberwocky.
Urban, Linda. (2011). *Hound dog true.* Harcourt Children's Books.

I No Longer Find It Funny. . .

KATIE WALKED TO SCHOOL, clutching her heavy books. She wished she could carry them in a backpack, but it was not cool for a fifth-grade girl to wear a back pack.

Dreading the climb to her second-floor classroom, Katie trudged towards the school's main entrance. Out of the corner of her eye, she noticed her friend Staci also struggling with the weight of her books as she hurried along. Katie was just about to yell to Staci, "Slow down or you'll fall," when Staci did just that.

Unable to use her arms for balance, Staci landed on her knees with papers flying everywhere and her books open on the pavement.

Of course, there were lots of kids around at that time of morning, and several of the boys from their class were close enough to see poor Staci crawling around on her hands and knees, trying to collect her things and to keep from crying.

A few of the boys laughed out loud, and some of them snickered and stared. None of them went to help.

Katie immediately hurried over. She did not hesitate as she helped Staci to her feet and gathered the rest of her papers and books.

Katie looked at the boys from her class and said, loud enough for all of them to hear, "Isn't it interesting how some people find it easy to laugh about something that most people no longer find funny. Some people just never grow up!"

The boys said nothing and quietly entered the building. Later in the morning, Katie noticed that one of the boys who had laughed asked Staci if she was OK.

That night Katie found her old backpack and put all her books in it to carry to school. Then she asked her sister if she could borrow an old one of hers to lend to Staci. Staci took it from Katie and was grateful. She used the backpack for a while, then, one morning, returned it and showed Katie the new one her mom had just bought her. It was big enough to carry all her books, was in the school colors, and had a place to keep a water bottle. Katie loved it and asked where she could buy one just like it. Staci said, "No need, I got you one too—as a present for being so nice."

Katie learned that growing up for her meant making good decisions. Using a backpack might not have been cool, but it was the smart thing to do. Katie thought about it and decided she would rather be smart than cool. Come to think of it. wasn't it cool to be smart?

By the following week, most of the students in the fifth grade were using backpacks again. This included the boys.

Discussion Guide

Title: ***I No Longer Find It Funny***

Family Member: Katie

Themes: Respect, Kindness

Summary: Katie watches her friend fall while other students laugh.
                      She decides she can help and starts a new school trend.

Standard: Health Education Standard 2
                      Student will analyze the influence of family, peers, culture,
                      *   media, technology and other factors on health behaviors.*

Objectives: At the completion of the lesson, the student shall:
- Recognize attributes of a true friend
- Describe how it feels to be embarrassed
- Compare behaviors that are acceptable with those that are inappropriate.

Pivotal Questions: Why did Staci fall?
                        How did Katie react when she saw her friend fall?
                        Why was Katie angry with the boys watching Staci?
                        What did Katie do to prevent Staci and her from falling?
                        Was this a good idea?

Evaluation: Evaluation shall be in terms of the student's ability to
                      recognize an unsafe as well as humiliating experience.

Teaching Strategies: Read the story through.
                         Read again asking pivotal questions.

Have students relate embarrassing situations they saw or experienced. Ask how they handled it or would have handled.

Allow students to write or role play an embarrassing scenario.

Follow-up Readings:

Bugbird, Tom. (2009). *My life unzipped.* HippoBook-DB.

Wasserman, Robin. (2009). *Ooops! I did it Again.* Scholastic, Inc.

I Could Have Told The Truth

KATIE BIT HER LIP to keep from crying. As she hurried home, she thought, Why didn't I just tell Staci that I couldn't go skating because I don't have the money? She would have understood. Instead I made up a lie about it being my mother's birthday, and that I had to bake a cake and all our relatives were coming over.

Staci knows I really don't have a big family of relatives. Katie felt certain that Staci knew she was lying. Staci was her best friend and would have understood, but Katie had just been too embarrassed to admit the truth.

Katie really wished she could go skating with Staci and the other girls. Staci's mom had offered to drive, and it would have been a great night, but she would need money to rent skates, and for pizza and ice cream afterwards. That was just impossible. Katie started to cry now and couldn't stop.

She slowed her walk so she could compose herself before getting home. She knew that, once she reached it, there would be no time for self pity. She had things to do around the house to help out. She wished she could live like Staci or any of her other friends. They all had *two* parents living with them—and a lot more money.

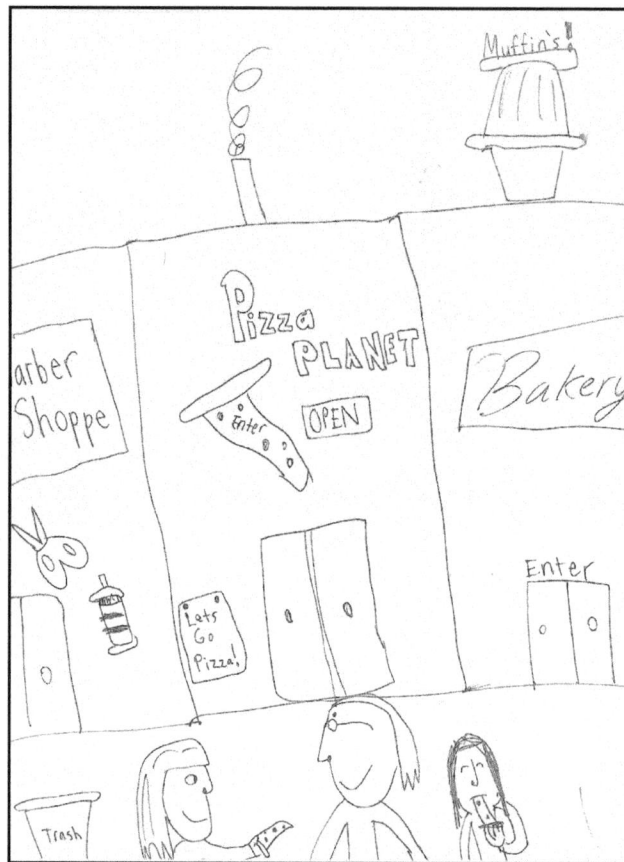

By the time she got home, she was cried out. As Katie was hanging up her coat, her mom yelled, "Staci's mom called. Did you tell Staci it was my birthday and you had to stay home?

Why did you lie?" Katie shrugged. Couldn't her mom figure it out? "Well, get your work done quickly. They're coming to pick you up in an hour. Staci's mom said this was her treat for being such a good friend to Staci."

Katie was ready and waiting outside in less than an hour. As she slid into the front seat of the car, Staci's mom whispered, "I'm *so* glad you could come. When I was your age, my family never had money for going out. Please let me know if you ever need help with money or anything else. You're a great girl and a good friend to Staci, and we love having you join us. You'll always be our guest—and never worry about money again!"

Katie bit her lip again to keep from crying with tears of relief and joy.

Discussion Guide

Title:	**I Could Have Told the Truth**
Family Member:	Katie
Themes:	Honesty, Compassion
Summary	Katie is too embarrassed to tell her friend that she can't go skating with her because she doesn't have the money. She makes up a phony excuse but finds it's not necessary.
Standard:	National Health Education Standard 4 *Students will demonstrate the ability to use interpersonal communication skills to enhance health and avoid or reduce health risks.*
Objectives:	At the completion of the lesson, the student shall: • Recognize that people will appreciate good qualities in people • Identify trusted adults who will help them • Appreciate that honesty will be rewarded • Choose friends who will support their needs
Pivotal Questions:	Do you think that Staci knew the real reason Katie couldn't go skating? Do you think that Katie's mom knew why Katie lied? What would you have done if you were Katie? Would you have told the truth? Do you think Staci's mom understood? Why did Staci's mom want to help? How do you think Katie demonstrated that she was a good friend to Staci?

Evaluation: Evaluation shall be in terms of the students' ability to empathize with Katie and relate it to their personal experiences.

Teaching Strategies: Read the story.

Re-read the story and ask the pivotal questions:

Allow students to answer the question, *Are there ever good reasons to lie?*

Have students write what they consider a good lie or bad lie.

What makes a good friend? How many really good friends do you have?

Are you a good friend?

Ask students to write whether they would rather be a good friend or have a good friend.

Follow-up Readings:

Mass, Wendy. (2010). *11 Birthdays, A wish novel.* Willow Falls Publisher.

Mass, Wendy. (2013). *13 Gifts, A wish novel.* Willow Falls Publisher.

Michael

The Right Thing

MICHAEL RAN HIS FINGERS along the upper shelf of his locker, hoping to find the small wallet he had hidden there earlier in the day. It wasn't there. With growing fear, he checked the lower part of the locker, hoping it had fallen onto his books, sneakers, or other items at the bottom. He still found nothing.

He frantically began to empty the stuff in the locker onto the floor, separating the items with growing anxiety, praying that, somehow, the wallet had hidden itself amid all the stuff.

No luck—the money was gone, stolen. Michael slumped to the floor right there in the middle of the hallway, too upset to even cry. He had deliberately hidden the money in his locker and made sure the combination lock was on securely. He had no idea how they had opened it or why he was always being targeted. He did know that, if he carried money around, those guys would corner him in the bathroom or somewhere and take it from him.

Sure they'd stolen from him before: bus fare or lunch money. But this was over a hundred dollars, money he had scraped together for the class trip he really wanted to go on. The entire class was going, and he didn't want to be left out.

If he told his mom, he was sure she would want to know why he had allowed the smaller amounts to be taken from him and failed to report it to the school. Why? He didn't know himself. Only that he didn't want to cause trouble, and that squealing would certainly make things worse. . .but this was just about as bad as it could get.

As he began replacing things in the locker, he heard footsteps. Glancing up, he noticed Cathy, the pretty cheerleader captain and the gang leader's older sister.

"Here it is," she said, handing the wallet back to him.

Michael grabbed it and checked, finding five twenty-dollar bills still tucked neatly inside. "What. . .how—"

"Please don't ask," Cathy insisted. "My brother and the other guys are in the principal's office now. This time they went too far. The police are coming to the school. My parents are leaving work to come here, too. My brother will have a lot of explaining to do."

"Thanks, Cathy. I'm. . .I'm sorry you had to get involved."

"Me too, but sometimes we all just need to do the right thing."

Discussion Guide

Title:	**The Right Thing**
Family Member:	Michael
Themes:	Honesty, Citizenship
Summary:	Michael is used to getting picked on. School is a place he feels unsafe in and is lost as to how to handle the bullies. After losing a large amount of money, he finds that an unexpected person has the strength to help him.
Standard:	National Health Education Standard 2 *Students will analyze the influence of family, peers, culture, media, technology and other factors in health behaviors.*
Objectives:	At the completion of the lesson, the student shall: • Define "bully," "victim," "character," and "integrity." • Describe the feelings associated with being bullied. • Identify reasons one might be bullied. • Recognize the difficult decisions one must make.
Pivotal Questions:	Why was Michael upset? How did Michael know whom to blame? Why was he unwilling to report the theft? Why did they repeatedly victimize him? What made Cathy report her brother? What might happen to her brother? What might happen to Cathy?
Evaluation:	Evaluation shall be in terms of students recognizing the no-win

situation the victim confronts and seeing the important role they have as bystanders.

Strategies:	Have students read the story and role-play the parts. Ask students to write a reaction paper taking the part of Michael, the bully or Cathy. Write the scenario from Cathy's point of view or her parents'.

Follow-up readings:

Modifica, Lisa. (June 2016). *Josh's Story—Getting Bullied at School.*

Daren. (2015). *Real Teens Speak Out: Stories from Teens like You, My Story and Advice.*

A Smile Crossed His Face

A SMILE CROSSED JOE'S FACE when he saw Michael enter the cafeteria. Joe poked his best friend, Antonio, and whispered, "Watch this." He lifted his backpack from the floor and dropped it on the only available seat at the table.

Carrying his tray, Michael approached the lunch table designated for freshmen and asked, "Can I sit here?"

Joe shook his head and said, "Sorry, no room."

In a faltering voice, Michael asked, "W-why can't you move your backpack and let me sit here?"

"Look, the table is too crowded, and we have no room for you, Michael the Moron. My backpack is more important than you, and I want it on that seat. You can sit on the floor or go with the girls, where you belong."

Joe and the rest of the boys at the table roared with laughter.

Joe was clearly the designated class leader. He was good-looking, smart, athletic, and already had girls who really liked him. When Joe said something funny, everyone laughed. Where he sat, the others followed. Joe chose the people he wanted to sit near him and set the mood of the day. That day, he was choosing to belittle Michael.

The other ninth-grade boys had had their turn. Now they seemed content to watch the torment continue, relieved they were not the brunt of Joe's cruelty.

Humiliated, Michael turned to leave and sit at an empty table. Antonio caught his eye and felt terrible. Michael and he had just finished working together on a science project, and Anto-

nio had been happy when the teacher teamed them up, knowing that Michael was smart and kind, and would be a great partner. He'd come to really like Michael and hated the way Joe was treating him.

But Antonio didn't know what to do. If he stuck up for Michael, he would no longer be part of Joe's group, and this is where he wanted to be. But he'd never *pick* on Michael, or anyone, the way Joe and the other guys did. Wasn't that enough? Michael had to learn to take care of himself. Antonio wasn't his mother.

He saw Michael sitting alone, looked again at Joe enjoying the moment, and suddenly, before he even realized what he was doing, he shouted, "Move your backpack *now* and let Michael sit here!"

Stunned, Joe barked, "I'm not moving anything. What are you going to do about it?"

"Look, Joe," Antonio said evenly, "I'm sick and tired of watching you be mean to guys. If you don't move it, I'm going to sit with Michael."

"Go ahead—now there are *two* morons." This time the other boys did not laugh with Joe. They sat in silence, waiting to see what would happen.

The silence continued as Antonio carried his tray to Michael's table. A few seconds later, another boy stood up. "I'm sitting over there. See you later."

Silently, the other boys picked up their trays and joined Michael and Antonio. Joe finished his lunch alone.

The next day, lunch started out as usual. This time, as Michael approached the table, the backpack was on the floor and the seat was available. When he sat down, he glanced at Antonio. A smile crossed his face, and a tear welled up in his eye.

Discussion Guide

Title: **A Smile Crossed His Face**

Family Member: Michael

Themes: Self-Discipline, Integrity, Prejudice

Summary: Michael is frequently the target of bullies, but none is more persistent than Joe, the designated school leader. One day, Joe is confronted and learns a lesson.

Standard: National Health Education Standard 4
                    Students will demonstrate the ability to use interpersonal communication skills to enhance health and avoid or reduce health risks.

Objectives: At the completion of the lesson, the student shall:
- Define what a bully is.
- Recognize the injustice of prejudice
- Appreciate the uniqueness of each individual
- Identify characteristics of the victim.
- Recognize that strength lies in the bystanders
- Plan how to respond to a bullying situation

Pivotal Questions: What do you think Joe was planning to do to Michael when he came into the lunchroom?
                    Why did the other boys laugh?
                    How did Michael feel when he was told he could not sit with the other boys?
                    Why didn't Michael throw the backpack off the seat and sit down right away?
                    What might the other boys actually be thinking?
                    What would you have done if you were at that table?

Evaluation Means:	Evaluation shall be in terms of having a meaningful discussion.
Teaching Strategies:	Read the story. Allow students to reread with volunteers reading or role playing parts of students. Ask students to share stories when they were bullied or witnessed a bullying incident.

Follow-up Readings:

A Heart-Touching Story of Friendship. https://mischievouseyez. wordpress.com/2013/01/24.

Frankel, Erin. (2015). *Nobody: A story about overcoming bullying in schools.* Free Spirit Publisher.

Rue, Nancy. (2014). *You can't sit with us.* Thomas Nelson, Inc.

Vanderberg, Hope. (2012). *Vicious: True stories by teens about bullying.* Free Spirit Publishers.

The Turning Point

MICHAEL HATED SCHOOL. He hated school, the teachers, his classmates, and most days his family as well. He knew he was different, but so were some other kids—yet they seemed to have friends and fit in better than he did. He wanted no part of after-school activities and hurried home immediately. Once he got to his room, he felt terribly lonely but safe.

Most days he didn't feel safe. Some teachers had excellent control of the class, and for at least a little while, he didn't have to worry about kids taunting him. But there were teachers who didn't care about students' behavior, and certainly not him. And there were always the hallways, the bathroom, or the locker area, too. Lunchtime was unbearable. Whenever he was out of the view of anyone in authority, he knew he'd be shoved, tripped, or ridiculed in some way.

There was no one to complain to either. Mom had her own issues, and Dad made it clear he wanted no part of Michael. He hated his parents too, especially his dad.

Michael gathered his books, closed his locker, and went into his homeroom. And so began another horrible day of his sophomore year, or so he thought.

As he entered the classroom, Michael noticed that his homeroom teacher was in the hall, talking to Mrs. Connelly, the drama coach. A few minutes later, the homeroom teacher asked Michael to step into the hall to speak with the coach. At first, Michael thought it was some kind of joke, but he had the drama coach for English class, and he seemed like a pretty cool guy.

Michael stepped into the hall and was immediately greeted warmly. "Michael, I need your help. I'm trying to put together the fall theater group, and I desperately need people to help out. I have you in mind for one of the major roles. Please come after school and try out. If you don't want to perform, there are so many other jobs available to do. I just want good, reliable people.

Michael couldn't believe his ears. Someone wanted *him* to be a part of a group activity with other kids. He nodded and said he'd be there. He really looked forward to working with a group. Mrs. Connelly handed him a script and told him to look it over to see if he preferred any one part.

Michael used his lunchtime to read the script and thought he resembled the lead. It was a long shot, but he decided to give it a try.

That afternoon, he read for the lead against three other guys. They joked and laughed while they waited their turn. Each one said nice things about the other's reading. Michael did a great job and actually wasn't surprised when he got the role. It would mean hours of work, but he could do it.

The play, and his performance, were a huge success. Michael was sad when it was over, but by then had a small group of friends he enjoyed spending time with. The bullying also stopped—for him, anyway. And when he saw others being tormented the way he had been, he felt confident enough to speak up.

Soon he began to look forward to coming to school. Michael was still different, and he knew he would always be. Only now he liked himself—and others did, too.

Discussion Guide

Title: **The Turning Point**

Family Member: Michael

Themes: Respect, Integrity

Summary: Michael is sad and lonely, and feels he just does not fit in until, one day, a teacher turns his life around.

Standard: National Health Education Standard 4
Students will demonstrate the ability to use interpersonal communication skills to enhance health and avoid or reduce health risks.

Objectives: At the completion of the lesson, the student shall:
- Recognize that all people experience periods of loneliness.
- Choose opportunities to be involved with peers.
- Select and seek out friends who support them.
- Develop a personal, no-bullying code of conduct.

Pivotal Questions? What issues in Michael's life contributed to his loneliness?
Why was Michael an easy target?
Could Michael have handled his life choices better?
Could other students have helped him?
Why was Michael so happy to try out for the Drama Club?
What is now different about his life?

Evaluation: Evaluation shall be in terms of the student's ability to relate to Michael's feelings and develop strategies to cope better themselves and help others to do likewise.

Strategies: Have a student read the story. Reread the story and pause to ask the pivotal questions.

Follow-up readings:

Levine, Irene. (2011). _It's tough making new friends in high school._

***

How to Make New Friends in High School. (2015).Wiki How to do anything. Retrieved on line.

Samantha

Hey, Baby

"**H**EY, BABY, WHAT ARE YOU doing after school today?"

"I have to clean the house, start supper, do homework—nothing special."

"Good, then it's a perfect day for me to come to pay you a little visit. I've never been inside your house, and I want to see your room."

"No, no, *please!* You can't come to my house."

"Why?"

"Because my sister and brothers will be out, my mother is at work, and no one'll be home till about 7:00.

"Perfect. That should work out fine. I'll *leave* before 7:00."

"...My mom doesn't let me have anyone over when they're not home."

"I'm not *anyone*. I'm your boyfriend, for three months now. We've only been alone a few times. It seems like I only see you in class with loads of other people around. It's time we got to know each other better, and today is the perfect opportunity.

"...But I'm only sixteen, and I'm not allowed to be alone in the house with *anyone.*"

"How come?"

"My mom's afraid we'll fool around."

"Fine. Then I'll bring a friend, and you get a girlfriend, so we won't be alone. We can just have something to drink, and you can show me your room."

"I'm afraid. I don't want to get in

trouble. *You* could get in trouble, too!"

"Get in trouble for *what?* Visiting a friend after school? I could be helping you with math. But look, if you don't trust me and want me for your boyfriend anymore, that's OK. I forgot you're a such a baby. . . . Am I coming to your house today or not?"

"No. I'm sorry."

"Fine. Then I'll give your friend Ashley a call. She always wants to see me, and no one bothers us in her basement.

"No! Please don't go by Ashley. You can come but only for a little while, and you can't bring beer.

"I promise I won't *bring* beer. Don't worry, no one will find out and we'll have a lot of fun."

"My mom wouldn't think this was fun."

"Good, she won't be there. I have a quick stop to make at the drugstore first. Write down your address, so I can have something delivered for us.

"OK. You and the delivery man should come to the back door. Here's my address."

"Thanks, baby. See you later."

"See you later, Mr. Johnston."

Discussion Guide

Title:	**Hey, Baby**
Family Member:	Samantha, high school junior, 16 years old
Themes:	Self-Discipline, Trustworthiness
Summary:	Samantha has become infatuated by someone who is not good for her. She must make a difficult decision.
Standard:	National Health Education Standard 7 *Students will demonstrate the ability to practice health-enhancing behaviors, and avoid or reduce risks.*
Objectives:	At the completion of the lesson, the student shall: • Recognize that not all adults have good intentions • Predict that some behaviors are too risky and carry heavy consequences • Create strategies to deal with difficult decisions
Pivotal Questions:	Does Samantha really care about Mr. Donnelly? Does Mr. Donnelly care about Samantha? Do you think Samantha wants Mr. Donnelly to come to her home? Why does Samantha give in and allow him to see her in her home, alone? Why does Mr. Donnelly need to stop at the drugstore? What is being delivered to her home? How does Samantha feel about herself?
Evaluation Means:	Evaluation shall be in terms of a meaningful discussion and the

student's ability to recognize that people will exploit them and they must make decisions for themselves.

Teaching Strategies: Have the students read the parts for Samantha and her boyfriend.
Follow with discussion and pivotal questions.
Provide an opportunity for counseling in and out of the school environment.
Discuss consequences for both Samantha and her teacher.

Follow-up Readings:
Locate and discuss news articles on inappropriate teacher–student relationships
Discuss consequences for both parties.

How Could You Do Such a Foolish Thing?

Samantha was a fool. She was also very much in awe of her new boyfriend and really thought she loved him. She would do anything to show him how much she cared.

She'd walk past the classroom she knew he was in and pretend not to notice him. Sometimes, she would wear her jeans low and her tops real tight so he would stare at her. The thought of him noticing thrilled her.

In school, he was always polite, but Samantha wasn't sure he cared about her the same way she did about him.

One day she had a brilliant idea. She was home alone and decided to take a picture of herself and send it to him, telling him how she felt. Maybe he just didn't know how much she cared. If she told him, maybe he would think of her differently.

She took a picture of herself lying on her bed, lipstick on and showing what she could of her sixteen-year-old breasts. She wrote, *Hi, been thinking of you. Do you ever think of me?* She attached the picture and sent it to him.

He immediately texted back, *Sure, I would love to see more of you.*

Samantha could feel her heart beating and quickly responded, *How about after school? We can walk home together.*

He responded, *I had something else in mind first. Send me another picture.*

She sent one of her face, up close, with her lips framed for kissing. Excitedly, she sent it off.

He did not respond for two days. She was heartsick. He avoided her at school, and every time she saw him he was with a different girl.

Samantha thought of trying to speak with him, but no opportunity came up. When he did finally respond, he asked for another picture. This time he wrote, *How can you stand wearing such a hot sweater? Take it off, so I can see what you really look like. All my girls like to show off what they have. I think you have even more, but I want to be sure before I date you.*

Samantha hesitated. She shook her head and thought, I can't. But if she didn't, she knew she'd never hear from him again.

She pulled off her sweater and bra, combed her hair, put on lipstick, held up her cell, took the picture, and sent it off before she could change her mind. She dressed herself and waited. There was no response. She felt as though someone had kicked her in the stomach.

The next day at school, she was de-termined to speak with him. She hurried into homeroom and immediately sensed that something was different. Her classmates stared at her but were silent. When the bell rang, the homeroom teacher asked to speak with her privately. "Samantha," she said, "a picture of you has been posted on the internet. You need to speak with the principal immediately." And then the teacher added, in a trembling voice, "How could you *do* such a foolish thing?"

Discussion Guide

Title: **How Could You Do Such a Foolish Thing?**

Family Member: Samantha

Themes: Integrity, Respect

Summary: Samantha's boyfriend demands she do something that she knows is wrong. Now Samantha must deal with the consequences.

Standard: National Health Education Standard 5
Students will demonstrate the ability to use decision-making skills to enhance health.

Objectives: At the completion of the lesson, the student shall:
- Describe how a bad decision has bad consequences
- Recognize the legal and moral implications of her actions, and the pros and cons of sexting
- Explain how her decision will impact her life long- and short-term

Pivotal Questions: What made Samantha pursue her boyfriend?
Why did she decide to send the picture?
What else could she have done to get his attention?
Was her boyfriend in love with her?
What do you think will happen to Samantha now?
How did her teacher feel?

Evaluation Means: Evaluation shall be in terms of a meaningful class discussion.

Teaching Strategies: Have students read the story.

Allow one to narrate and others read parts of Samantha and boyfriend.

Discuss what will the likely outcome be.

How will Samantha handle this embarrassment?

Follow-up Readings:

YouTube videos: *Sexting at School, Dangers of Sexting: What Teens Need to Know*

I Never Told Anyone This Before

"**I** NEVER TOLD ANYONE this before," said Samantha as she looked into Mary Beth's soft brown eyes and at her clear beautiful skin, and warm, braces-filled, toothy smile. But Samantha caught herself. She knew she must not share the information with her new neighbor. Samantha was about to disclose a family secret—burdensome information for a sixteen-year-old girl. It was a deep dark secret, and one she had to keep. . .especially with someone she had really just met.

What she was about to say would hurt her brother deeply and could destroy her mother, but it was burning to come out. Mary Beth seemed like a trustworthy friend, and Samantha needed one badly.

The night before, she'd heard her brother Michael crying in his room. He had tearfully confided in her that he thought he was gay. She'd listened with a heavy heart, agonizing for him. After he talked for over an hour, she'd looked him in the eye and said, as clearly as she could, "Look, Michael, you're only thirteen years old—far too young to know for sure if you are or are not gay. Why do you have to face this *now?* You're a terrific guy, and I think you're just perfect the way you are, gay or not!"

He had smiled at that and thanked her—and Samantha had promised to keep his secret. Before leaving his room, she had said, "Look, if you need anyone else to talk to, I'll find you help. For now, I think you shouldn't worry about something you can't change. We'll deal with this if we have to."

It was the first time Samantha had hung out alone with Mary Beth. She didn't know her very well but wanted to. Once the secret was out, maybe Mary Beth would share something of her own, something close to *her*, and their friendship would be secure, stronger than that of other eleventh-grade girls. It would be so wonderful to have someone to talk to.

But Samantha had promised her brother.

"What? What is it you never told anyone before?" Mary Beth asked.

Samantha held her breath. "...I can't remember!"

Disappointed, Mary Beth shrugged. "Oh, OK. No big deal"

Samantha walked home upset, alone, and very sad. She climbed the back steps quietly. She was not in the mood to talk to her mom or anyone else. She was headed for the solace of her room and diary. As she closed the door, she heard the muffled voice of her mom on the phone in the next room and was relieved she hadn't heard her come in.

After dinner, Samantha went through her closet, trying to find some-thing to wear to a party that week end. How hard it was to make such a simple decision when there was something hurting you inside. But she was proud of herself for not betraying her brother.

The phone rang. It was Mary Beth. "I know what you wanted to tell me be-fore."

Samantha froze. "Really? What do you mean?"

"You're lying to me, and friends don't lie to each other." Samantha was silent. "My mom was talking to your mom just now. I heard my mom tell the scout leader not to let my brother go camping with *your fag brother*. I am not allowed to hang out with you either."

Stunned and with robotic ease, Samantha hung up the phone, put her clothes back in the closet, and lay down on the bed. She would not be going anywhere for a while.

Discussion Guide

Title:	**I Never Told Anyone This Before**
Family Member:	Samantha
Themes:	Trustworthiness, Integrity
Summary:	Samantha has a hidden family secret. She resists the temptation to betray the confidence but learns that someone close to her does just that.
Standard:	Health Education Standard 2 *Students will analyze the influence of family, peers, culture, media, and technology, and together factors on health behaviors.*
Objectives:	At the completion of the lesson, the student shall: • Define what it is to be a friend • Demonstrate appropriate behavior regarding confidences • Compare Samantha's behavior with that of her mother • Support the rights of privacy for all • Analyze Samantha's behavior • Evaluate the impact of the secret on her brother
Pivotal Questions:	Why was Samantha so desperate to have a friend? What held her back from sharing the secret? Why do you think her mother told Mary Beth's mom the secret? How do you think Samantha feels now about the adults in her life? What impact will this have on Michael?
Evaluation Means:	Evaluation shall be in terms of having a meaningful class

discussion and the ability for students to relate to the characters.

Teaching Strategies: Have students read the story. Allow them to speak parts of Mary
Beth and Samantha.

Discuss with the class:

Friendship: what does it mean?

How do you know if someone is really a friend ?

What is gossip? Is it beneficial?

Have the class list the characteristics of a friend.

Break the class into several groups. Allow each group to
prioritize the traits they feel are most important.

Have each group defend their choices.

Follow-up Readings:

Whitney's Story, www.best-friends-forever.com.